TEACHER JOKES

Compiled and Illustrated by
Viki Woodworth

Printed in the United States of America.

Distributed to Schools and Libraries
in the United States by
ENCYCLOPAEDIA BRITANNICA EDUCATIONAL CORP.
310 S. Michigan Avenue
Chicago, Illinois 60604

Library of Congress Cataloging-in-Publication Data
Rothaus, James.
Teacher jokes / Jim Rothaus; compiled and illustrated by Viki Woodworth.
p. cm.
Summary: A collection of jokes and riddles about teachers, including
"What is a math teacher's favorite kind of dancing? Square dancing."
ISBN 0-89565-725-2
1. Teachers–Juvenile humor. 2. Questions and answers–Juvenile humor.
[1. Teachers–Wit and humor. 2. Schools–Wit and humor. 3. Jokes. 4. Riddles.]
I. Title. 91-17080
PN6231.S3R68 1991 CIP
818'.5402–dc20 AC

TEACHER JOKES

Compiled and Illustrated by
Viki Woodworth

THE CHILD'S WORLD

Teacher: Charlotte, I will have to ask your father to come and see me.
Charlotte: You'll be sorry. He's a doctor and charges $50 a visit.

Teacher: Why does the ocean roar?
Student: Well, wouldn't you if you had crabs on your bottom?

Charlie: Teacher, I just swallowed a pencil.
Teacher: Keep calm and be happy.
Charlie: Happy? About what?
Teacher: That you didn't swallow a book bag.

Teacher: How could you divide 10 potatoes evenly between 7 people?
Student: Mash them.

Teacher: Give me a sentence with a direct object.
Student: Teacher, you're gorgeous.
Teacher: What's the object?
Student: An "A."

Where did Napoleon keep his armies?
Up his sleevies.

Teacher: Why did George Washington cut down the cherry tree?

Pupil: Gosh, I'm stumped.

Teacher: Define the word "disease."
Student: "Disease" is de grade below the Bs.

Child: I'm not going back to school tomorrow.
Mom: Why, dear?
Child: "Well, I can't read and I can't write and they won't let me talk, so what's the use?"

Teacher: Where was the Declaration of Independence signed?
Student: At the bottom.

What does the science teacher feed his pet frog?
Croakers and milk.

What's so nice about kindergarten teachers?
They know how to make little things count.

Teacher: How can you be such a perfect idiot?
Student: I practice a lot.

What is an English teacher's favorite dance?
The Oliver Twi

Principal: Do you believe in clubs for children?
Teacher: If nothing else works.

Teacher: Which ant is the biggest?
Student: A giant.

What kind of food do math teachers eat?
Square meals.

Teacher: Sally, be quiet. The people next to you can't read.
Sally: They should go back to first grade.

Student: Hooray! The teacher says we'll have a test today, rain or shine!
Other Student: Why are you cheering?
Student: It's snowing!

Teacher: What conducts electricity?
Pupil: Why . . . er . . .
Teacher: Correct, wire conducts electricity. Now, what is the unit of electrical power?
Pupil: The what?
Teacher: Right, the watt.

Teacher: Which ant is the meanest?
Student: A tyrant.

Teacher: This homework is in your father's handwriting.
Student: I know, I used his pen.

Teacher: Did you take a bath today?
Student: Why, is one missing?

Teacher: What did they do at the Boston Tea Party?
Student: I don't know. I wasn't invited.

Teacher: How can you keep fish from smelling?
Student: Put on noseplugs.

How did the messy student write his paper?
With his pigpen.

Teacher: Why do bees hum?
Dolly: Because they don't know the words.

Why did the teacher give Molly dog biscuits?
She was teacher's pet.

Andrew: Teacher, I think I'm becoming a highway!
Teacher: What's come over you?
Andrew: Two trucks, one bus, six cars and a motorcycle, so far.

Teacher: How long is a minute?
Student: What kind of minute? A real minute, or a "wait-a-minute"?

Teacher: If I had 15 oranges in one hand and 3 in the other, what would I have?
Student: Big hands.

Student: I et six eggs for breakfast.
Teacher: You mean, "ate."
Student: Well, maybe it was eight.

Where do math teachers soak in the evening?
In the math tub.

Student: I don't deserve a zero on this test!
Teacher: I know, but it's the lowest grade I can give.

Why did the creature take so long to finish the 10-page book?
He wasn't very hungry.

Teacher: Pat, what do you mean crawling into school 3 minutes late?
Pat: You said not to dare ever walk in late.

Teacher: Are you late again?
Student: Yes, teacher, but didn't you say it's never too late to learn?

Teacher: Joe, this is your 19th mistake today. How can you manage it?
Joe: I got up early.

Why did the teacher marry the school janitor?
He swept her off her feet.

Teacher: Who is Homer?
Student: The guy Reggie Jackson made famous.

What kind of dog does a science teacher prefer?
A laboratory retriever.

Why did the pioneers go west in covered wagons?
They didn't want to wait 40 years for a train.

Teacher: Can you define pasteurized?
Student: When something is too far to see.

Teacher: What nationality is Santa Claus?
Student: North Polish.

Teacher: Matt, name one important thing we have today that we didn't have ten years ago.
Matt: Me!

Ted: I didn't sleep well last night.
Teacher: Why not?
Ted: I plugged my electric blanket into the toaster and kept popping out of bed all night.

Teacher: What don't you like to eat at breakfast?
Student: Dinner.

Where does every math teacher go in New York City?
Times Square.

Teacher: Which end of a worm is the head?
Student: I don't know. Let's tickle him and see which end smiles.

Teacher: Did the Indians hunt bear?
Student: Not in winter.

Teacher: How many bones do you have in your body?
Student: 1000.
Teacher: 1000!
Student: I had fish for lunch.

Teacher: How do you spell "wrong"?
Student: R-O-N-G.
Teacher: That's wrong!
Student: Good, I got it right.

Teacher: What did they wear at the Boston Tea Party?
Student: T-shirts.

Why is the letter "A" like a flower?
Because "B's" come after it.

What do you call a math teacher who always says "I'll do it later"?
A calcu-later.

Teacher: What did Benjamin Franklin say when he discovered electricity?

Student: Not a word. He was too shocked.

What do you call someone who teaches the recorder?
A tooter (tutor).

Teacher: Would you rather lose your life or your money?
Student: My life, I'll need my money for my old age.

Teacher: Paul, what are you thankful for this Thanksgiving?
Paul: I'm thankful I'm not a turkey!

Teacher: Please tell me the definition of ignorance.
Student: I don't know.
Teacher: Very good! That's correct.

Teacher: Alex, do you find it hard to make decisions?
Alex: Well–yes and no.

Teacher: I hope I didn't see you looking at Brian's paper.
Student: I hope you didn't either.

Teacher: What kind of bird is this?
Student: A canary.
Teacher: Canaries aren't green.
Student: Maybe it's not ripe yet.

What did the librarian keep as a pet?
A cat-alog.

What letter can sting you?
The "B."

What's the difference between a teacher and a doughnut.
You can't dunk a teacher in a glass of milk.

Substitute Teacher: Are you chewing gum?
Pupil: No, I'm Sammy Smith.

What's the difference between a train and a teacher?
One says "Choo-choo" and the other says, "Take the gum out of your mouth."

Teacher: You didn't do your homework!
Student: It's my mother's fault! She forgot to nag me.

Teacher: What famous words did Paul Revere say on his horse?
Student: Giddy-up?

Teacher: Johnny, have your eyes ever been checked?
Johnny: No, teacher, they've always been brown.

Teacher: I'm so pleased I can give you a "B" in math!
Student: I bet you'd be *thrilled* if you gave me an "A."

Why does a math teacher comb his hair?
To get out the rectangles.

Where is the center of gravity?
At the "V."

Teacher: Tyler, please name 7 wild animals.
Tyler: Three bears and four lions.

Teacher: Why is your name "$6\frac{7}{8}$"?
Student: My dad picked my name out of a hat.

Teacher: Annie, do black cats really bring bad luck?
Annie: If you're a mouse they do!

Where do math teachers eat?
At the lunch counter.

Teacher: You're late. Why?
Student: I obeyed the sign. It said, "School ahead, Go Slow." So I did.

Teacher: Will, do you know the 18th President?
Student: No, we never met.

Why do teachers take aspirin?
For de-tension headaches.

Which ant flunked out of school?
The ignorant.

Teacher: Peter, who is the youngest in your family?
Peter: My gerbil.

What is green and slimey and teaches school?
The teacher from the Black Lagoon.

Teacher: Why do bells ring at Christmas?
Student: Because someone pulls the rope.

Teacher: I have tiny pupils.
Doctor: Are you sick?
Teacher: No, I'm a kindergarten teacher.

Teacher: Do you know, "London Bridge is falling down"?
Student: No, can they fix it?

Teacher: Tell me what is a digital computer?
Student: Counting on my fingers.

Why did the teacher go outside with her purse open?
She expected some change in the weather.

What is a math teacher's favorite kind of dancing?
Square dancing.

Teacher: If you don't stop all that racket, I'll go crazy!
Student: Too late, Teacher. We stopped an hour ago.

Teacher: How do you like doing homework?
Student: I like doing nothing better.

Teacher: You're late! You should have been here at 8:00.
Student: Why? What happened?

Teacher: Why was George Washington buried at Mount Vernon?
Student: Because he was dead.

Student: I haven't slept in 7 days!
Teacher: Aren't you tired?
Student: No, I've been sleeping at night.

Teacher: How can you start a fire with two sticks?
Student: Make sure one is a match.

Teacher: Billy, what are the four seasons?
Student: Soccer, football, basketball, baseball.

Student: I think the school cook is a bully!
Teacher: But why?
Student: I saw him whip cream and beat eggs!

Teacher: Megan, you should take something for that cold!
Megan: The rest of the week off?

Teacher: There is a fire burning in your body all the time.
Girl: I know. When it's a cold day I can see the smoke.

Student: My science teacher says I should be an oceanographer.
Dad: Really, why?
Student: Because all my grades are below C level.

Teacher: Why did you swallow that money?
Student: It was my lunch money.

Teacher: Why is there a Mother's Day and a Father's Day, but no Son's Day?
Pupil: Because there is a Sunday every week.

Teacher: If we breathe oxygen in the daytime, what do we breathe at night.
Student: Nitrogen.